FIRST-GLANCE FINANCE

Investing Your Money

B. J. Best

Cavendish Square
New York

Published in 2015 by Cavendish Square Publishing, LLC
243 5th Avenue, Suite 136, New York, NY 10016

First Edition

Website: cavendishsq.com

CPSIA Compliance Information: Batch #WW15CSQ

All websites were available and accurate when this book was sent to press.

Library of Congress Cataloging-in-Publication Data

Best, B. J., 1976-
Investing your money / B.J. Best.
pages cm. — (First-glance finance)
Includes index.
ISBN 978-1-50260-103-2 (hardcover) ISBN 978-1-50260-273-2 (ebook)
1. Investments—Juvenile literature. 2. Finance, Personal—Juvenile literature. I. Title.

HG4521.B4475 2015
332.6—dc23

2014024965

Editor: Amy Hayes
Senior Copy Editor: Wendy A. Reynolds
Art Director: Jeffrey Talbot
Senior Designer: Amy Greenan
Senior Production Manager: Jennifer Ryder-Talbot
Production Editor: David McNamara
Photo Research by J8 Media

The photographs in this book are used by permission and through the courtesy of:
Cover photos by Lana K/Shutterstock.com; Juan Camilo Bernal/Moment Open/Getty Images; Lana K/Shutterstock.com, 1; lendy16/Shutterstock.com, throughout; Goodluz/iStock/Thinkstock.com, 5; Express Newspapers/Hulton Archive/Getty Images, 7; tupungato/iStock/Thinkstock.com, 9; Burke/Triolo Productions/Photolibrary/Getty Images, 11; Zack Blanton/Vetta/Getty Images, 13; Lambert/Archive Photos/ Getty Images, 15; Christofer Dracke/Thinkstock.com, 17; david franklin/E+/Getty Images, 22; DNY59/ E+/Getty Images, 25; YinYang/E+/Getty Images, 26; JGI/Jamie Grill/Blend Images/Getty Images, 30; Peter Gridley/Stockbyte/Getty Images, 32; Howard Berman/Stone/Getty Images, 33; Ronnie Kaufman/Larry Hirshowitz/Blend Images/Getty Images, 36; larry1235/Shutterstock.com, 37; Hill Street Studios/Blend Images/Getty Images, 39; Syda Productions/Shutterstock.com, 40; JGI/Jamie Grill/Blend Images/ Getty Images, 41.

Printed in the United States of America

CONTENTS

ONE / 4
What Is Investing?

TWO / 10
Why Do People Invest?

THREE / 16
The Math of Investing

FOUR / 24
The Pros and Cons of Investing

FIVE / 29
The Best Ways to Get Started

SIX / 35
Your First Investments

GLOSSARY / 42

FIND OUT MORE / 45

INDEX / 46

ABOUT THE AUTHOR / 48

CHAPTER ONE

What Is Investing?

What would you do if someone gave you $100? Would you buy a toy or game? Would you give it to your family to help pay for food? Would you give it to a friend who might need it, or to a charity that helps others? Maybe you would save that money, hoping that you would earn even more later.

When people take money they have today and use it to try to have more money in the future it is called investing. Investments are an important part of our

Families can meet with financial advisors to decide the best ways to invest their money.

economy. They help a business get the money it needs, especially when it needs to buy something that is expensive. They also help the government raise money necessary to run programs and build important things such as roads and schools.

Most importantly, investments can help people save money for big **expenses**, such as a vacation, car, college education, or house. Investments can also allow older people to retire and live off of the money they saved throughout their lives.

Investments can be as simple as putting money in a bank. They can be as complex as buying the right to sell a certain **commodity** at an agreed-upon price at a certain time in the future. Today, investments occur in many different ways. People can even make investments in countries other than their own.

The History of Investing

People around the world have been investing money for a long time. The Code of Hammurabi is one of the earliest set of laws that has been preserved. It is estimated to have been written about 3,700 years ago in

Long-Ago Legislation

Two specific laws from the Code of Hammurabi are: "102. If a merchant entrust money to an agent (broker) for some investment, and the broker suffer a loss in the place to which he goes, he shall make good the capital to the merchant. 103. If, while on the journey, an enemy take away from him anything that he had, the broker shall swear by God and be free of obligation."

The New York Stock Exchange is a very busy place where hundreds of millions of shares of stock are bought and sold every day.

ancient Babylonia, which is now within present-day Iraq. It contains several laws about investing to ensure that everyone involved is treated equally.

In the first days of the United States, citizens found ways to invest in their new country. Some people made investments by starting **companies**, or officially established businesses. These businesses produced many different goods such as iron, chocolate, and clothing. Other people made investments by purchasing **shares of stock** in some of these companies.

A share of stock represents a small ownership of a company. When the company does well, the value of the share of stock increases. The first, and best-known,

IPO: Ready, Set, Go!

An initial public offering, or IPO, is the first time all interested investors have an opportunity to purchase shares of stock. When successful companies announce an IPO, many investors try to be among the first to buy shares so that they can buy as many as possible. For example, Google first offered shares of stock in its company for sale to investors on August 19, 2004. People invested $1.67 billion in Google that day!

marketplace for buying and selling stocks in the United States is the New York Stock Exchange, a form of which was first established in 1792.

Investing Today

Today people invest in many things, including natural resources such as gold, oil, and land. They also invest in farms and food. Investors can buy and sell things such as grain, corn, cattle, soybeans, coffee, and sugar.

Owners of stocks were once issued certificates like these. Today, it is becoming more common for an owner to have an electronic record instead.

People continue to invest by creating their own companies. Someone who starts a company must purchase equipment, such as machines or supplies, and must hire people to work for the company. Recently, there have been many successful companies in computing businesses, such as Google. Just like early Americans, people can invest in these companies by buying shares of their stock.

People can invest by depositing money in the bank. The bank uses the money for its business, and pays a fee, known as **interest**, to use that money. There are different types of accounts at a bank, and they pay different amounts of interest. If someone agrees to deposit money in a bank for a long time, they will earn a higher amount of interest.

There are many different ways people can invest their money so they will have more money in the future. Investments help the American economy grow. They can also help people achieve financial goals for their lives.

CHAPTER TWO

Why Do People Invest?

Why do businesses need money from other people to operate? Why can't they use money they already have?

Imagine you want to start your own business. If it's summer, a lemonade stand might be a good idea. What expenses do you think your business would have? What would you have to spend money on before you could begin to sell lemonade?

A lemonade stand is a popular way for kids to begin investing and understanding the choices investors need to make in a business.

You would certainly need lemonade ingredients. You'd need a pitcher to make the lemonade. You'd need cups for the lemonade when you sell it. You would need a table or booth. You would also probably want a sign that says you have lemonade for sale and how much it costs. You might even want a few more signs to hang around your neighborhood to advertise your business.

All of these items cost money. You might be able to get some of these supplies from home. But imagine if you had to buy everything before you began. Suppose the total cost was $20, but you only had $10. Where could you get the other $10? By asking people to invest in your business!

How Businesses Get Money

There are several different ways people could invest. For example, you might ask your aunt to give you a **loan** of $10 today to buy your supplies. However, you would be expected to repay that $10 at a later time. You would also be expected to pay some interest. You might agree to repay the $10, plus an extra $1, in a month. Your aunt would receive $11. The extra dollar is her reward for investing in your business.

You might ask your friend Stacy to join in your business. If she has $10 and you have $10, together you can take $20 and buy your supplies. This is called a partnership, where both of you would agree to divide everything evenly. When your lemonade stand makes money, you would give half of that money to her. That's her reward for helping you start your business.

You could even create your own stock. You could sell a share of stock for $1. If you sold one share to ten friends, you would have enough money. Each friend would then own a small portion of your business. By selling stock, you would agree to give a small amount of the money you make, known as a **dividend**, to each person who bought a share of stock. If your business does well in a week, for example, you might pay each owner 10¢.

Risk Versus Reward

Different investments appeal to different people. People's goals and personalities influence how they invest. One important factor is how much risk people like to take.

Taking bigger risks give investors the possibility of earning larger rewards. But it also increases the possibility of facing larger losses!

In investing, this is known as risk versus reward. The riskier something is, the more people want to be rewarded for it. For your lemonade stand, the riskiest choice would be invest all of your own money, without outside help. Let's say there's a hot stretch of weather and you have a lot of customers. You would get to keep all of the money you made selling lemonade, which is a good reward.

However, if your business did poorly, you could lose much of your money. What if a strong wind came

The Tart Tycoon

Lemonade stands have been around for a long time in the United States. Children were selling tart, refreshing lemonade to thirsty travelers as early as the 1870s in New York City. One of the first known children was Edward Bok, who was ten when he sold ice water for a penny per glass. In his autobiography, *The Americanization of Edward Bok*, he describes his transition to lemonade: "One Saturday the young ice-water boy found that he had a competitor; then two and soon three. Edward immediately met the challenge; he squeezed half a dozen lemons into each pail of water, added some sugar, tripled his charge, and continued his monopoly by selling 'Lemonade, three cents a glass.' Soon more passengers were asking for lemonade than for plain drinking water!"

Kids have been running lemonade stands in the United States for over one hundred years. As the price of ingredients has gone up, so has the price of lemonade.

through and blew over your stand? Lemonade would spill. The pitcher might break. Signs might blow away. If you don't have more money, you might not be able to continue your business. That's why running your own business is high risk, but can also be high reward.

It's less risky to have Stacy as your partner, but there is also less reward. You would get to keep only half of the money you make, but you would only lose half as much money, too. In our example, the stockholders of your business have the least risk of all. If your business closes, they only lose $1. On the flip side, if it does well, they only get paid a small amount. They don't have much risk, but they also don't have much reward.

CHAPTER THREE

The Math of Investing

Math is important in investing. By using math, people know how much money their investments are making. They can also tell if they've made good investments.

Percentages

A key math concept for investments is the **percent**. "Percent" means "by the hundred," and is indicated using the "%" symbol. Any percentage can be written as a fraction over 100. For example, take 12%. That means 12 percent, or 12 "by the hundred," and can be written as:

It is very important to understand the math of investing, because it determines how much money investments gain or lose.

$$\frac{12}{100}$$

43% can be written as

$$\frac{43}{100}$$

and 2% can be written as

$$\frac{2}{100}$$

Percentages are used to tell how much money an investment should earn. A low percent means an investment earns less money overall, while a higher percent means more money. Remember risk versus reward, however. An investment with a higher percentage might make more money, but it is also probably riskier!

Percentages are important because they establish the interest rate. The interest rate determines how much interest, or extra money, an investment earns above its original amount. Interest rates are used in loans and other investments.

Paying Interest

Imagine you need $10 to run your lemonade stand. Your friend Carlos is willing to lend you that $10. He would expect you to pay a fee since you are using

A Symbol's Source

Why does the "%" symbol look the way it does? "Per cent" is originally a Latin phrase. In Italian, it became ***per cento***, which still means "every hundred." In the fifteenth century, when people abbreviated per cento, they wrote it like this: ***p c***^{o}. By the seventeenth century, it began to look like this: ***p o/o***. Soon, the "***p***" was dropped, leaving the "***o***" both above and below a line, which evolved into our current "%" sign.

his money. That fee is known as interest. Carlos will charge you a 10% interest rate, and expects you to repay the loan in a month.

How much money are you paying in interest? First, write 10% as a fraction:

$$\frac{10}{100}$$

To calculate the interest, multiply the amount you have borrowed by that fraction. You borrowed $10, so multiply ten dollars by 10%:

$$\$10 \times \frac{10}{100} =$$

A whole number is just itself divided by 1, so set up the equation as:

$$\frac{\$10}{1} \times \frac{10}{100} =$$

Now if you multiply the numerators and multiply the denominators you get:

$$\frac{\$10}{1} \times \frac{10}{100} = \frac{\$100}{100}$$

How do we change this from a fraction into a whole number? We simplify:

$$\frac{\$1\not{0}\not{0}}{1\not{0}\not{0}} = \frac{\$1}{1} = \$1$$

That means you owe $1 in interest. So, when you repay the loan to Carlos in a month, you would have to repay the original amount, known as the **principal**, plus the interest. You would pay $10 principal plus $1 interest. That makes the total amount you'd repay $10 + $1 = $11.

Earning Interest

Let's look at an example where you would earn interest. Most banks sell an investment called a **certificate of deposit**, which is abbreviated "CD." A CD is similar to a savings account, but requires you to

Even Fractions Add Up

What if Carlos instead charged you a 20% interest rate? Do you think you'd pay more or less interest? The interest is the principal times the interest rate. That would be

$$\$10 \times \frac{20}{100} = \frac{\$10}{1} \times \frac{20}{100}$$

Multiply the numerators and the denominators:

$$\frac{\$10}{1} \times \frac{20}{100} = \frac{\$200}{100}$$

Simplify:

$$\frac{\$200}{100} = \frac{\$2}{1} = \$2$$

You would repay the principal plus the interest: \$10 + \$2 = \$12. When you are charged a higher interest rate for a loan, you will have to repay a higher amount.

leave your money at the bank for a certain amount of time. In exchange for letting the bank keep your money for that time, the bank will pay you an interest rate. Banks can sell CDs that **mature** in as little as one month, or as long as five years.

Imagine you bought a $50 CD that will mature in one year. The bank will pay you 8% interest. What is the interest you earn, and how much total will the bank pay you in one year? The interest rate is

$$\frac{8}{100}$$

Your principal, or starting amount, is $50. The total interest is then

$$\$50 \times \frac{8}{100} = \frac{\$50}{1} \times \frac{8}{100} = \frac{\$4\cancel{00}}{1\cancel{00}} = \frac{\$4}{1} = \$4$$

The total the bank will pay you is $50 + $4 = $54.

Let's imagine a different CD where you invest $200 at an interest rate of 10% for one year. After one year, the bank would pay you the interest of

$$\$200 \times \frac{10}{100} = \frac{\$20\cancel{00}}{1\cancel{00}} = \$20$$

Your total amount would be $200 + $20 = $220.

Now, you could take that money and do what you would like with it. However, imagine if you invested it again. You would invest $220 at a 10% interest rate. How

Compound interest allows small amounts of money to grow into much larger amounts over time. The earlier someone invests money, the larger it can grow.

much money would you have after another year? The interest would be

$$\$220 \times \frac{10}{100} = \frac{\$2200}{100} = \$22$$

Your total amount would be $220 + $22 = $242.

Investing the interest you have earned is called **compound interest.** It is a very powerful idea in investing because it allows your money to grow over time. In fact, if you were to invest $200 and leave it in the bank for ten years, you would have over $500!

Remember that percents are fractions out of 100. An interest rate is a percentage that a loan will charge or an investment will earn. A higher interest rate means more money, but could also mean more risk. Interest rates are important in evaluating investments.

Compound Interest

Year	Principal	Interest Rate	Interest Earned	Total at End of Year
1	$200.00	10%	$20.00	$220.00
2	$220.00	10%	$22.00	$242.00
3	$242.00	10%	$24.20	$266.20
4	$266.20	10%	$26.62	$292.82
5	$292.82	10%	$29.28	$322.10
6	$322.10	10%	$32.21	$354.31
7	$354.31	10%	$35.43	$389.74
8	$389.74	10%	$38.97	$428.72
9	$428.72	10%	$42.87	$471.59
10	$471.59	10%	$47.16	$518.75

CHAPTER FOUR

The Pros and Cons of Investing

Investing can be a good way of growing money over time, but it can also be risky. What are some positive aspects of investing? How should people be careful when investing?

Advantages of Investing

People invest for a lot of reasons, but they usually can be summarized as only one: to make money. People usually don't invest to make a few dollars. They invest to try to

401(k) plans allow people to invest for their retirement. In these plans, people can choose to invest in stocks, bonds, and mutual funds, among other investments.

have large amounts of money. One very common reason for people to invest is for their retirement. When people work, they have a steady flow of money they can use for daily expenses. When people retire and stop working, that flow of money also stops. People then can use their investments to provide money.

A common way to invest for retirement is through a 401(k) plan. A 401(k) plan is a retirement account offered by many businesses for their employees. A worker can choose to have money subtracted from her paycheck and invested into this plan. Sometimes companies will even match this investment. For instance, if I invest $50, my company would also give me $50 to invest.

However, you can't use the money until you reach age 59½. The plan is meant for retirement savings only.

People invest for other large expenses, too. You could invest in a special plan that can only be used to pay for college education known as a Section 529 plan. People might invest so they can buy a house or a car, or enough money to go on a nice vacation.

Goals help determine how and where to invest your money.

You can also invest to have money available for unexpected events. These events could be good or bad. For example, people are often excited to have a new baby. However, you might be surprised to learn that it costs about $12,000 to raise the baby for the first year!

Risks of Investing

Investing does have some risks. One common concern with investing is **opportunity cost**. When you invest your money, it means you can't spend it anywhere else. For example, once you've invested your money in a 401(k) for retirement, it stays in that investment until you retire. Later, you might have the opportunity to buy a car at a great price with that money, but you can't. The law prevents you from using your money until you retire.

Some investments can lose money. This is especially true for stocks. The price for a share of stock in major

Save Today, Retire Tomorrow

401(k) plans were first offered in the early 1980s. The name 401(k) refers to the section of U.S. tax law that allows the plans to be created. In 1982, only a few large employers offered these plans. However, they quickly became a popular way for employees to save for retirement. Thirty years later, in 2012, more than 51 million Americans had a 401(k) plan. Together, they had $3.5 trillion in investments!

companies changes every day. Sometimes its value goes up, and sometimes it goes down. When you buy a share of stock, there is no guarantee its value will ever increase.

Sometimes the price of many stocks can suddenly go down. These losses have caused trouble for the United States several times in history. In late October 1929, the U.S. stock market lost over $30 billion in just two days. This began the Great Depression. Many people lost a lot of their money in their stock investments. Some people lost almost all the money they had. The Great Depression was a time when many people could not find work. Those who did have a job often worked for less money, and couldn't afford things necessary to live.

Fluctuating Funds

Although some stocks can lose money, the stock market has been the best investment over time. Since 1975, the U.S. stock market has increased in value by about 10 percent every year—but that doesn't mean it grows steadily. The best year was 1975, when values increased by 38 percent. The worst year was 2008, when values decreased by 33 percent.

In the late 1990s people were excited to invest in the stocks of Internet companies. These companies sold goods on the Internet, and also provided online services. The Internet was new, and people wanted to invest in these companies. They thought they could make a lot of money. Many investors didn't think about which companies would truly make money in the long run. A lot of these early Internet companies failed, and investors lost all of the money they had in their stocks.

Overall, investments are a good way for people to increase their money for future expenses. People can choose how risky they'd like to be with the money they invest. Investing allows people to lead comfortable and productive lives now and in the future.

CHAPTER FIVE

The Best Ways to Get Started

Your Goals

To begin investing, you should determine what your goals are. Do you want to invest money so you can pay for college? Do you want to start your own business? Do you want to have money for a large purchase, such as a car when you turn sixteen? Some of these ideas might seem like they're years away, but the earlier you can begin investing your money, the better.

You should also ask yourself how comfortable you are with risk. Remember that risk and reward are linked. Would you like your money to grow at a slower rate, but have its value guaranteed? Or would you like to have a chance to make more money, with the risk that your investment might decrease in value?

You should also ask when you might need the money in your investment. **Liquidity** is how easily an investment can be turned into cash. Cash is the most liquid investment, since it is already cash—but it also earns no interest! Money in a savings account is very liquid, because all you have to do to get cash is go to the bank and withdraw it. However, many investments require your money to be in that investment for a certain period of time. It could be months or many

College is a large expense for most people. It's a good idea to begin investing for college as soon as possible, even if it's just a small amount at a time.

years. Other investments can only be used for certain expenses, such as college or retirement plans.

Your goals, your feelings toward risk, and your timeline will help determine the right type of investments for you.

Savings Bonds

One common investment for young investors is a U.S. savings bond. By purchasing a savings bond, you are giving a small loan to the U.S. government. The government will then pay you interest. You can buy a savings bond for as little as $25. You must hold on to the savings bond for at least one year. After that year, you can **redeem**, or cash in, your bond for its original value plus its interest. It will continue earning interest for up to thirty years. Since savings bonds are backed by the U.S. government, they are very safe investments. Since they are safe, though, they earn a low interest rate.

Stocks and Mutual Funds

Perhaps you are interested in buying stocks. Stocks are usually liquid, as they can be sold quickly for cash. Remember, though, that purchasing shares of stock in an individual company can be risky. Values of individual stocks can change a lot from day to day. It's a good idea to purchase stock in a company only if you know a lot about it, and you are confident it will make money in the future.

Bond Beginnings

Savings bonds were designed for new investors without a lot of money. The first savings bond was sold on March 1, 1935. The minimum price was $18.75. Because these were small investments, they became known as “baby bonds.” Many people bought the bonds, which allowed the government to begin programs that helped end the Great Depression. Today, savings bonds are the most widely held investment in the world.

If you like stocks, a better idea for young investors would be to invest in **mutual funds**. A mutual fund is a collection of several different investments. Mutual funds can invest in stocks, land, and loans. A mutual fund is considered safer than an individual stock because it spreads the risk around. If you own stock in one company and that company fails, you lose all of your money. A mutual fund might own stock in that company as well as stock in fifty other companies. If one company fails, the mutual fund will lose some money, but it will not lose all of its money.

This man is being quite risky with his eggs, baskets, and chickens.

By spreading its investments across many companies, the mutual fund is **diversified**. Have you ever heard the expression, "Don't put all your eggs in one basket"? That's because if the basket breaks, all the eggs will break. Diversified investments spread out their risk. Each egg is in a different basket. That helps prevent losing all your money.

Protecting Your Information

A final important idea as you begin investing is to carefully protect your personal information.

Reducing the Risk

How many stocks should someone own to spread out risk? Experts have different opinions. Most people agree a diversified investment is between twenty and thirty stocks. A mutual fund, on average, has about 150 stocks. About 54 million households in the United States own a mutual fund, and 93 percent of those people say one of their goals is to save for retirement.

Your personal information is anything that identifies who you are on official forms. This includes your name, address, telephone number, and Social Security number. Many investments will require this information so you can show you own the investment. However, you should never give your personal information to someone you don't know. Criminals can take your information to commit crimes.

CHAPTER SIX

Your First Investments

You might think you're too young to start investing. In fact, the perfect time to start investing is when you're young. Remember compound interest. The earlier you start investing, the sooner you can also invest that interest. If you invested $100 now at a 10 percent interest rate per year, and kept that investment for 50 years, by the time you would retire you would have almost $12,000!

You might also think you don't have a lot of money to invest. Even small amounts can add up over time, however. Could you set aside $5 every month? At the end of the year, you'd have $60, which you could invest.

You can use money you've saved in your piggy bank to buy investments such as savings bonds.

If you earned an 8 percent interest rate each year, you would have almost $1,000 after ten years.

Buying Savings Bonds

One of the easiest and best investments for kids is U.S. savings bonds. They cost as little as $25, and you can redeem them in as little as one year. Savings bonds are considered to be risk-free, since they are guaranteed by the U.S. government. There are two types of savings bonds you could buy: "EE" or "I." An EE bond has a clear interest rate. An I bond has an interest rate that

Which Bond's a Better Buy?

Because the interest rate on an I bond changes, it's difficult to say which bond is a better investment. An EE bond guarantees the value of the bond will double at twenty years. If you bought a $25 EE bond, it would be worth $50 after twenty years. Some people recommend if you are going to hold onto a bond for less than twenty years, buy an I bond. For an investment lasting twenty years or more, buy an EE bond.

can change. Both are safe investments that guarantee you will not lose your money.

Savings bonds are often used to save for college expenses. If you redeem your savings bond to pay for college, you might not have to pay taxes on the interest you earned. You would be making money without having to pay it to the government.

Savings bonds are now purchased and redeemed online, and are very easy to buy. You can be the owner of a savings bond, but you'll need an adult to open an account for you and buy the savings bond.

Getting Advice

It can be more complicated to buy stocks or mutual funds. If you're interested in these investments, the best thing to do would be to talk to a financial advisor. Financial advisors work at banks and investment companies and help others decide how to invest. You could ask your parent or guardian to set up an appointment with an advisor. The advisor would talk to you about your goals and your feelings toward risk. Then they would make some recommendations for your investments.

There are also some websites which allow people to buy and sell small amounts of stock. You can ask your parent or guardian to search for these websites and open an account at one. Remember that stocks have a potential to earn more money than other investments. However, they are also riskier, and their value can go down.

Some kids make money by running their own lawn care businesses. They offer services such as lawn mowing, raking, and weeding.

Your Own Business

Of course, you could invest money in yourself by being an **entrepreneur**. An entrepreneur is someone who runs his or her own business. Some common businesses that kids can start are lemonade stands, lawn care services, and dog walking. You would have to decide what equipment and supplies you would need. You would also need to be motivated to keep your business going, especially if you are the only person in your business.

Running your own business is a great way to take responsibility for your money. Every business you visit was started by someone. Starting your own business can be a great way to achieve success. Businesses can be risky, though, so you'll want to carefully plan how you spend your money so you can make more than you spend.

Online Business Options

The Internet has also given kids new areas to start their own businesses. If you know a lot about computers, you might be able to start a business helping others run their computers better. If you know how to design websites, many small companies might be able to use your help. Some blogs look for kid-created content, and they might pay you for your writing.

The best time to start investing is when you are young. Compound interest can help your small investments grow into large ones over time.

Now Is the Time to Start Investing

You are in a great position. Most people don't think about investing until it's late in their lives. The earlier you start, the more interest you can earn, which means you'll have more money later. It's never too early to start investing, and there are no amounts that are too small to invest. By investing, you can help make sure you will have money for future expenses. You will be able to live the life you want.

GLOSSARY

certificate of deposit (CD) A deposit at a bank for a certain length of time.

commodity A food or natural resource that is bought and sold.

companies Officially established businesses.

compound interest Earning interest on interest that has been invested.

diversified When risk is spread out over many investments.

dividend A small payment received from a share of stock.

economy The making and using of all goods and services in an area.

entrepreneur Someone who starts a business.

expenses Things people spend money on.

financial advisor A person who has the job of suggesting how people should invest their money.

interest A fee charged for loaning money.

liquidity How easily an investment can be turned into cash.

loan Money given to someone that is expected to be paid back.

mature To complete the required time for an investment.

mutual funds A collection of investments sold as a single investment.

GLOSSARY

opportunity cost When you use money for one purpose, you can no longer use it for anything else.

percent A fraction out of 100.

principal The original amount of a loan.

redeem To cash in.

share of stock A small ownership of a company.

FIND OUT MORE

Books

Minden, Cecilia. *Investing: Making Your Money Work for You.* Ann Arbor, MI: Cherry Lake Publishing, 2008.

Morrison, Jessica. *Everyday Economics: Investing.* New York, NY: Weigl Publishers, 2010.

Rumsch, BreAnn. *Economy in Action!: Saving & Investing.* Minneapolis, MN: ABDO Publishing, 2012.

Thompson, Helen. *Junior Library of Money: Investing Money.* Broomall, PA: Mason Crest Publishers, 2011.

Websites

Money as You Grow

moneyasyougrow.org

Learn key tips to being a smart investor and discover important topics to consider for any age.

The Mint

www.themint.org

This educational website offers sound advice for the new investor and much more.

Investor.gov

http://investor.gov/classroom/students

Get some advice from the experts at the U.S. Securities and Exchange Commission and find out how to invest in responsible and safe ways.

INDEX

Page numbers in **boldface** are illustrations.

401(k) plans, 25–27, 25

Bok, Edward, 14
bonds, **25**,
  baby bonds, 32
  EE bond, 36–37
  first sold, 32
  I bond, 36–37
  savings bonds, 31–32, **36**,
    36, 38

certificate of deposit (CD),
  19, 21
  maturity, 21
Code of Hammurabi, 6
commodity, 6
companies, 7–9, 26–27, 40
  in mutual funds, 33
  Internet companies, 27
  investment companies, 38
  matching investments, 25
compound interest, 22, **22**,
  35, **41**
  chart, 23

diversified, 33–34
dividend, 13

economy, 5, 9
entrepreneur, 39
expenses, 5, 10, 25–26, 31, 38
  future expenses, 28, 41

financial advisor, **5**, 38
financial goals, 9

goals
  financial, 9
  investment, 13, **26**, 29, 31, 38
  savings, 34
Google, 8–9
Great Depression, 27, 32

initial public offering (IPO), 8
interest, 9, 12, 18, 22, 35
  earning, 19–23, 30–31, 36, 38, 41
  owing interest, 19
  paying interest, 17–18, 20
  See also, compound interest; interest rate
interest rate, 17, 21–23, 36–37

lemonade stand, 10, **11**, 12–13, **15**, 17, 39
liquidity, 30
loan, 12, 17–20, 22, 31, 33

mature, 21
mutual funds, **25**, 31, 33, 38

New York Stock Exchange, **7**, 8

opportunity cost, 26

partnership, 12
percent, 16–17, 22, 28, 34–36
principal, 19–21, 23

redeem, 31, 36, 38
retirement, 25–27, **25**, 31, 34
reward, 12–13, 15
  high reward, **13**, 15
risk, 26, 29–31, 33–34, **33**, 38–39
  high risk, 13, 15, 22
  risk-free, 36
  versus reward, 13, 17, 29
  See also, opportunity cost

savings account, 19, 30
Section 529 plan, 26
share of stock, 7, 12–13, 26–27
stocks, 8, **9**, **25**, 26–28, 31, 33–34, 38

ABOUT THE AUTHOR

B.J. Best holds college degrees in finance and actuarial science from Drake University. He teaches writing at Carroll University in Wisconsin, where he has served on the Planning and Budget Committee. He enjoys helping his four-year-old son invest for college.